REMOVING THE MASK

REMOVING THE MASK

Stephanie R. Bullock

How My Wilderness Experience Blessed My Soul

Removing the Mask
Copyright ©2017 Stephanie R. Bullock
April 2017

MacKenzie Publishing
Halifax, Nova Scotia

ISBN-13: 978-1927529423
ISBN-10: 1927529425

Editor: C.A. MacKenzie
Cover design: Stephanie Rushworth

�ୠ
MacKenzie Publishing

Dedication

"For the Lord your God has blessed you in all that you have done:
He has known your wandering through this great wilderness.
These forty years the Lord your God has been with you; you have
lacked for nothing." (Deuteronomy 2:7)

To my husband, Reggie:
You cover me in all things. You had me at hello. My life and our
children's and grandchildren's lives are richer because you cover
us.

My brother, Stephen Malone:
I love you to the moon and back.

Carolyn, Bonita, Phyllis, and Stephanie:
Thanks for always covering me.

Richard L. Taylor, Jr., author of *Love Between My Scars:*
Thank you for connecting me to the phenomenal publisher
Cathy MacKenzie, who gave my story life.

My story is dedicated to all women who have gone through the
wilderness and removed the masks so their stories will be a
blessing to other women currently in their wilderness season.

Introduction

Mask: *A covering for all or part of the face,*
worn to conceal one's identity
(www.dictionary.com)

In writing this book about my wilderness season, I wanted to be raw and transparent for my sister girls.

Many women are not living their fullest lives because they are afraid to remove the mask out of fear of being judged by another woman—or even family.

For many years, there was shame attached to my story because I let others define it for me. Shame for me has turned to power. In sharing my wilderness experience, I want to remove the mask so other women reading my book understand that they are not alone going through this wilderness season. My wilderness experience is my testimony of God's faithfulness, grace, and mercies.

I no longer see myself in a distorted mirror based on what people have said or done to me. I now see myself through my Heavenly Father's eyes. I am one of God's Glamor Girls.

My prayer and hope for my sister girls are that they will release the shame of their stories and know their beauty is magnified when the mask comes off.

Stephanie

Table of Contents

Family Secrets

My entire life I felt like a motherless child. I was born on July 12, 1967, in Chicago, Illinois, to Verletta Malone and Michael Lawrence Malone. My mother had just turned nineteen on the day I was born. Yes, my mother and I share the same birthday.

I never met Michael, the man whose name appeared as father on my birth certificate. I was always told Michael married my mother while she was pregnant with me so that I wouldn't be born out of wedlock.

At the age of five, I learned my biological father was Albert Bailey, Jr., and not Michael Lawrence Malone.

As the family story goes, when my mother informed Albert that she was pregnant with me, he immediately said, "I am engaged to be married, and that baby isn't mine." My grandmother encouraged my mother to marry Michael Malone so my mother, being eighteen at the time, wouldn't have the stigma of an out-of-wedlock child. My belief is that my grandmother wanted my mother to marry Michael so that she— my grandmother—wouldn't be embarrassed. You see, my grandmother cared a lot about how her family was perceived by friends.

Five years later, Albert decided to come clean to his family regarding me being his child, and took me and my mom to meet his parents, who had just learned I was their granddaughter. I remember meeting my biological father's family for the time and was overjoyed because I had a DADDY!

However, Albert didn't have time to bond with me because he was murdered on New Year's Eve 1975 in Milwaukee, Wisconsin, while robbing a liquor store with a friend. You see, my father was a drug addict and living in Wisconsin because he was supposed to be in a drug rehab facility. I went to his funeral, not fully realizing what was happening, and never realized the impact his death would have on my life. But I would come to find out.

After Albert's death, I built a bond with his family. My paternal grandparents loved me unconditionally. Because I was my father's only child and the only remaining connection my paternal grandmother had of her only son, I believe she sincerely tried to get to know me.

My mother was diagnosed with renal kidney failure when I was five years old, and while my mother was in and out of the hospital, my brothers and I were passed from house to house.

At the age of seven, when my mom was having a dialysis treatment, I was dropped off at a cousin's house, where I was molested by a family member. I was awakened from a nap by that family member fondling my private area. I was afraid, and I felt so unprotected and alone. Later that evening, when I revealed to my grandmother what had occurred, she looked at me with an expression I will never forget and yelled, "Stop lying, Stephanie."

Throughout that year, I would continue to be dropped off into the hands of the enemy.

A Brief Moment of Happiness

The summer of 1976, I was sent to a camp in Williams Bay, Wisconsin, for two weeks. During the second week of camp, a counselor walked into my cabin, hugged me tightly, and said, "Stephanie, I am so very sorry, but your family is on their way to get you. Pack your bags." I wondered what I had done to be sent back home to Chicago.

Another counselor entered the cabin and said, "I am so very sorry, but your mom has passed."

My mother died on July 7, 1976, at the tender age of twenty-seven. While I took in the words "your mother passed," I felt as if my life had ended at that very moment. I remember the episode as if it was yesterday.

After my mother's funeral, I was informed my brothers and I would be living with my grandmother (the same woman who had handed me to the enemy who had molested me). While sitting in the front pew at my mother's funeral, I knew the mother's love I had experienced with my mom was forever gone, buried in the casket with her.

The Lion's Den

After settling in with my grandmother, I quickly realized that love for me didn't exist. My grandmother favored my brothers, and she reminded me on a regular basis that I was nothing and would never amount to anything. At times, she referenced me dying at an early age like my mother.

I never understood why she hated me so much. I thought if I was the perfect child, she would show me love simply because I longed for it. Grandma sent my brothers and me to church every Sunday morning, where we would stay through evening services. She loved the idea that people thought she was this perfect woman who took in her young grandchildren. I was always reminded I should be grateful she took us in because no one else wanted me.

During this time, while I sang my heart out in the young adult choir in church, I didn't think God knew me or loved me. There I was, a seven-year-old child singing, "Yes, Jesus Loves Me," but I didn't believe one word of that song.

As a child, I'd never been to a sleepover. Why, you ask? My grandmother made sure that if she kept me close, I wouldn't be able to remove my mask.

At the age of ten, I was informed by a family friend that my maternal grandmother wasn't really my grandmother but was actually my great aunt. When I asked my maternal grandmother about this, her response was, "I am your mother's mom and raised her since she was six months old. Don't ever question me again." I never mentioned this again until I became a teenager.

At the age of twelve, I moved in with my father's family. It was definitely during this time when I was given my freedom. My grandmother worked out an agreement with my father's parents that she would send $100 dollars a month for my everyday necessities. You see, when my mom died, my brothers and I received my mother's monthly social security.

I went crazy wild while living with my father's family. I was given so much love by my paternal grandmother.

My mother's mom later moved me back to her home because she became jealous of the relationship I had with my paternal grandparents.

The Enemy Comes to Kill and Destroy

After moving back into the home with my maternal grandmother, she continued to keep a strong grip on me, along with abusive words: "You'll never amount to anything," and "If I die, I do not want you at my funeral."

To escape her voice and to create another family in my mind, I oftentimes went down to the basement to listen to music. I was hungry for love. Even as a young girl, I always felt God had abandoned me. I couldn't wait to turn eighteen to escape my grandmother's harsh words. I was taught at an early age to wear the mask by my grandmother. She would say things to me like, "Steph, the girls are watching you, and if you make a mistake, you will be shamed."

Really? Who says that to a young child? As the years went by, I developed a strong coping mechanism in dealing with the abuse of her words.

One evening, I decided to approach my grandmother again with "Who is really my grandmother?" This conversation didn't go well. Once again, I was bombarded with her angry words, but

I received the answers I was searching for. I learned my biological grandmother was actually her sister, who had abandoned my mother at six months old because she and my biological grandfather were both heroin addicts.

I was crushed. What part of my life was the truth? It finally made sense why this woman, who I had thought for years was my biological grandmother, berated me with words the way she did.

Lies. Lies. Lies

During my senior year of high school, I met my high school sweetheart, a young man who was smart and popular and my escape from home life. After dating him for about a year, I discovered I was pregnant a couple of months before graduation. I decided I would tell him the news after prom.

I remember the day I told him as if it was yesterday. While he and I sat in my grandmother's living room, I uttered the words "I am pregnant." He responded, "Don't worry, we will be okay. We will get through this together."

The next morning, I watched out the front window for him to pick me up for school, which he did most mornings, but he never showed. I sat in my grandmother's living room and sobbed uncontrollably. I eventually walked to the bus stop to catch the bus. When I arrived at school, the seniors were in the auditorium for graduation rehearsal. I immediately spotted him and walked over. He told me he felt as if I was ruining his life because he was leaving for the University of Illinois in the fall.

I was devastated by his response. You see, this was the same individual who had said he loved me and would never leave me. Once again, I felt I was worthless of being loved. During this time, Satan started to deposit words of worthlessness in my spirit.

After I returned home, I entered the bathroom, opened the medicine cabinet, and downed a bottle of pills. I wanted to end the pain. After waking up at The University of Chicago hospital, surrounded by my paternal grandparents and with a tube in my nose, all I could do was cry.

When the doctor walked into the room, he informed my family that I would be okay. He also told them I was pregnant, which wasn't the way I wanted them to find out.

I was released from the hospital a few days later, but because I had tried to commit suicide, it was the state of Illinois protocol that I be transferred to an outreach mental health facility before I could return home. After arriving at the facility, fifty miles outside of Chicago, I went through the normal intake process and was assigned a roommate and counselor.

My counselor, Ms. Ford, was to the point and didn't hold punches when it came to making me realize how selfish I was. For once someone listened. I missed my high school graduation ceremony, and while my classmates celebrated with their families, I was in a psych ward.

I was released to my grandmother three weeks later. After returning home, my family scheduled an appointment for me to have an abortion. All I wanted was to move beyond what I had gone through and get a grip on my life.

I enlisted in the United States Navy during my junior year of high school through the delayed entry program. I left for boot camp on August 12, 1985. I was excited about being in the Navy because I felt I could finally hear those words "I am proud of you" from my grandmother. I not only had a lot to prove to everyone, but also to myself. Needless to say, even after completing boot camp, I never heard those words from my grandmother.

I soon realized that boot camp reminded me of all the negativity I had experienced while living with my grandmother. I had a company commander who always yelled in my face. Yelling, yelling, and more yelling!

I hated my company commander until the day I graduated from boot camp when she said, "Recruit, I am so very proud of you. The reason I yelled so much was because I was trying to break you down to build you into the woman who is standing in front of me today, just like the Heavenly Father does."

Wow! The woman who yelled for eight weeks was a Christian?

After leaving boot camp, I was assigned to a base in Meridian, Mississippi, for AIT school, where I met an officer named Jason. Jason and I went against military policy by dating. He was an officer, and I was an enlisted in AIT School. After a year of dating, I informed Jason I was pregnant. Jason said I couldn't have the baby because it would jeopardize his military career. Here we go again, I thought. Someone who stated they loved me really didn't love me at all.

After procrastinating for four months, my decision was pretty much made for me, because it was too late for an abortion. I immediately contacted Lutheran Child & Family Services in Chicago, where I was assigned a case manager named Gwen. Gwen quickly went into work mode to find a placement for the daughter I would give birth to. Six weeks later, when I was in San

Diego, Gwen called to tell me she had found a family who had already adopted a biracial child and wanted another.

I flew to Chicago a month later to meet Bob and Bonnie because this would be an open adoption. Open adoption meant I could keep communication open with the adoptive parents and could meet my birth daughter once she turned eighteen if she and I both agreed.

In November 1987, while home in Chicago on leave from the military, I was awakened by labor pains. I immediately dressed and drove myself to The University of Chicago hospital. My grandmother, who didn't want to be a part of this, refused to accompany me.

Without any family members to support me, I gave birth to a baby girl. The nurses cleaned up Emily and handed me this tiny, beautiful baby. I wasn't allowed to hold her, but they had forgotten I was placing her for adoption. While I held her, a myriad of emotions swept over me, including love, joy, disappointment, fear. You see, I felt I wasn't good enough for her.

When the nurses removed Emily from my arms, I felt as if my soul had been ripped away.

After I completed my time with the Navy, I moved back to Chicago for a brief period, where I obtained a job with the Marriott Corporation as a guest services agent. During that time, I met a gentleman, travelling for work, who was checking out of the hotel. We exchanged numbers and kept in touch over the next year.

Al lived in Maryland, about seven hundred miles away, but we decided to remain exclusive to each other, and I visited him several times during that period. On one visit, I decided to stay in Maryland and not return to Chicago.

Al and I had a son and a daughter together. He traveled a lot for work, and on while on one such trip to California, I found out he was having an affair with a woman there. Our son had just turned one when I discovered the affair, and I immediately left him.

Stripped of Everything in the Wilderness

I was living in Maryland without family and had way too much pride to return to Chicago to live with my grandmother. Also, home in Chicago represented pain.

I struggled with my babies. I worked but could barely make ends meet. After I hit rock bottom, I had no choice but to stay at a women's shelter (Shepherds Cove Shelter). God was setting me aside so I could hear His voice, even with background noises. I cried every night while at the shelter because I thought I was too good to be in such a place. Who in the hell did I think I was?

While at the shelter, women from Ebenezer AME Church came every Tuesday evening to have Bible study with the residents. One Tuesday evening, God spoke very clearly to my spirit. I made my way to Bible study, and the word these women of God brought forth changed my life. I finally understood I was set aside for a purpose.

The shelter helped me transition into housing, and I promised I would be back to volunteer and to speak life into another woman, so that she too would know she was set aside for a purpose. After moving out of the shelter, I returned every Tuesday to teach Bible study with Ebenezer (my church to this day).

One Tuesday evening while volunteering at the shelter, a beautiful sister said to me, "You are so put together, how would you know how we feel? We live in a shelter."

I took a deep breath, grabbed her hand, and stated, "Sis, I am you. I too was a resident at this shelter just a year ago."

As we both cried and hugged in the hallway, I knew my purpose was to be a beacon of light for others so they could see how God transforms. That woman I had witnessed to is now a general manager for Target stores and gave my daughter her very first job.

My Boaz

While I'd wait at the bus stop to go to work in the mornings, a black Acura would turn out of the townhouse development where I lived, and the driver would wave. I'd wave back.

One morning, the car made a U-turn. The driver stopped in front of me, and said, "Do I know you? Because you wave at me."

I replied, "You wave at me every morning."

I didn't know this man was sent by God and would not only be my husband, but would be an angel for me and those I loved.

After dating for about six months, he looked at me. "You shouldn't be riding the bus with your children." He purchased a vehicle for me so my children and I would have proper transportation. Who does that?

This man loved me even in my brokenness. He wanted the best for my children. I was so use to folk taking from me, and all he wanted to do was love me.

After three years of dating, we married, and my life truly came together. My husband, Reginald, saved me. He was not only my husband, best friend, and lover, but most of all he was my covering sent by God. My husband made me feel secure in removing the mask so I could be the best wife and mother for our family.

But I also knew I needed to deal with the hurts from my childhood. If not, they would manifest their way into my marriage, and I wasn't having that.

A Life Full Circle

Just when I was ready to have that truthful conversation with my grandmother about how she'd hurt me, she developed Alzheimer's.

Once a month, I flew home to Chicago to coordinate her care, everything from caregivers to paying her bills. I remember returning home one time from Chicago and telling my husband how tired I was of flying back and forth. He replied, "Babe, bring your grandmother here to live with us."

My response was, "Honey, you want me to do what? Do you not remember the pain she caused me?"

He wasn't having my excuses. All he knew was that my grandmother was eighty-five and had no family left in Chicago. He didn't care what had happened between her and me when I was younger; she needed me now. I reluctantly gave in, and we moved her into our home in Maryland.

Reginald and I were blessed with a caregiver, Tanya, who came into our home Monday to Thursday to take care of my grandmother while he and I worked. My husband and I rotated

going out on the weekends; one weekend I went out, and the next weekend he went out.

I felt as though I had given up my life to care for someone who had caused me much pain, but I became the mom and took care of my grandmother as if she were my child. I coordinated her doctor appointments, cooked her meals, and made sure she was bathed.

My children interacted with her. They loved her and she loved them. I was happy she was so loving with them, but I was sad at the same time. One evening, I broke into tears because my heart still harbored pain and unforgiveness, and she didn't remember any of it. I still wore the mask my grandmother taught me how to wear.

While I was washing her feet one evening, she looked at me and said, "Steph, I am so very proud of the woman you are. God always has a ram in the bush for us all, and you are my ram."

I never cried so hard in my life. God has a funny sense of humor, and the bondage was broken for me that very moment. My grandmother never wanted for anything while in my home. I became the mom and she became the child. I know God works out everything for our good.

My grandmother lived with my husband and me until her death at the age of ninety-three. She died with her hand in mine, and her loss affected me to my core. I thank God for bridging the gap of forgiveness for the two of us. When God is in the midst of our lives and situations, all things work for our good.

I love my husband to the moon and back for seeing the best in her even when I didn't. My grandmother loved him as if she'd birthed him. She died in our home knowing she was loved, and that burden was lifted because I knew she loved me. I mourned my grandmother's death harder than I thought I would have because just when I was able to truly love her, she was gone. I know God placed her in our home for a purpose.

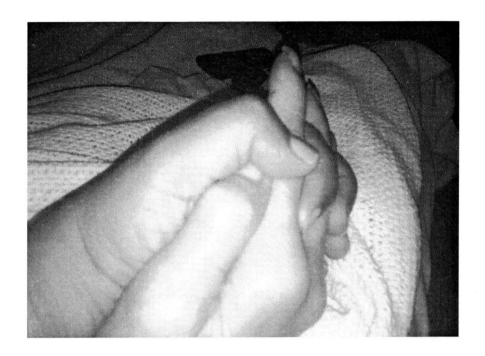

I still hear her voice saying, "Steph, what would I have done without you?" What she never knew was that I needed her more than she needed me. I needed her love, and I received that in the end. If I had to do it all over again, my grandmother would be right here with me.

My Heart is Restored

While in Atlanta for work one Tuesday evening, I received a phone call from Gwendolyn, the social worker at Lutheran Child & Family Services in Chicago.

She asked, "Stephanie, are you sitting down?"

"Yes, I am, Gwen," I responded. "Is everything okay with Emily?"

She informed me that Emily had just turned eighteen and wanted to meet me—her birth mom. Gwen asked how soon I could get to Chicago.

That Friday, I was on a plane from DC headed to Chicago. I was a nervous wreck, worrying about the questions Emily would ask about why I put her up for adoption. As I stood in the lobby of the Sheraton Hotel in downtown Chicago, a younger version of me walked in. We instantly hugged and cried and talked for hours. She told me about her life over the past eighteen years, and I sat in awe of this gorgeous young woman, who had turned into a great singer and athlete.

When the weekend ended, Emily looked at me and said, "I need you to know that giving me up for adoption was the most selfless thing anyone could have done, and I know you loved me."

Set Aside for a Purpose

ALL the time I thought I was in pain, I was in purpose. God had his arms around me through every uncomfortable life situation I had ever been in.

I'm no longer looking in a distorted mirror of what family and peers have said to me and about me. I see myself through my Heavenly Father's eyes. I am no longer ashamed or apologetic of my past and will not be bound by it. I am not a victim, but a survivor, for I am more than a conqueror.

My prayer is that a woman reading my story will realize that she is fearfully and wonderfully made, and no weapon, no attack, no assignment that is not of God shall prosper. Never let anyone shame you over your past. Your past is your experience, which qualifies you to pull out others.

It is so very important to not let folk convince you that they have always had it together, because that is furthest from the truth. They are afraid to take off the mask. When you are in your darkest hours, it so very important to learn to speak life into yourself and your situation. Remember, God will work it out for your good; just trust Him.

My purpose is to speak life and wholeness to the broken because I am qualified to do so. I am not qualified because of a degree or title; I am qualified because I have been deep in the wilderness and the fire, and I SURVIVED by the grace of God. I am now living my destiny, and destiny is when you know who you are and to whom you belong. I am a child of God and belong to him.

So many women walk around wearing masks. I removed the mask, and now I am free to LIVE and help others. You don't have to look like what you've been through. My prayer is that women will peel away the masks and share their testimonies because other women need to see how God transforms. I now know my Heavenly Father's voice, and I now listen only to HIS voice.

During my wilderness seasons, God was in every experience, every tear, every disappointment, every loss. God was sharpening me for a time such as this. I needed the sharpening to be able to share my story with those of you reading MY story now. I asked God, "Lord, how am I supposed to share the shame with folk?" At that very moment God asked me a question: "Are you ashamed of ME? Because I never left you." That was it for me, and I started writing and sharing my story.

I look back over my life and realize that God held my hand the entire time. I show compassion because I wasn't showed compassion. I love unconditionally because unconditional love wasn't shown to me. I forgive because forgiveness frees you. I also now realize that taking my grandmother into my home and caring for her while she was afflicted with such an awful disease like Alzheimer's was part of God's plan.

I am a witness that out of your greatest pain comes your greatest testimony. I removed that mask, and now I am free to LIVE and extend my hand to my sister girls with no judgement attached. I need my sister girls to know that they do not have to look like what they've been through.

(#BYTHEWORDSOFOURTESTIMONIES)

Our testimonies exalt God and embarrass the enemy. My prayer is that every woman will embrace her wilderness experience. God guided me through my wilderness experience, and it BLOWS MY MIND that I came out polished with love, forgiveness, and compassion—all because of HIS grace and mercies. I am so very grateful for God's hand on my life. God turned it all around for my god, and the Devil can't do anything about it.

Start sharing your stories, ladies. The year 2017 is all about #HERstoryinthemaking. I don't judge my sister girls because I don't know what God is birthing in them and through them, but I now know God was birthing something great in me even as a child.

It is so very important that you know there is purpose to every wilderness season we endure. God is equipping you. Ladies, it's time to remove the masks. Another woman needs to see how she can go through the wilderness and come out polished. "For I know the plans I have for you" (Jeremiah 29:11).

Write the vision; make it plain. Never let anyone shame you over your past. Your past is your experience and identifies who you are, which now qualifies and equips you to help another woman. The woman I am today now understands that my wilderness season wasn't bad, because God was in every experience.

Sister girls, please stop judging other women. Love yourself first so that you can learn to love your sister girls. Ladies, we all have a story. I am an extension of my sister girls. Ladies, lift your heads, wipe those tears, fix your crown, and ROCK IT OUT! Remember to bless another sister with your story so she will know and see that you can go through the fire and come out polished. Because I have experienced the grace of God, I now cover my sister girls instead of exposing them.

My testimony is: I've stumbled; I've failed; I've been talked about; I've lost; I've been hurt; but I GOT UP, thanked God, and helped another sister girl so that God will get all the Glory. My testimony is greater than myself because what should have broken me positioned me to break through barriers.

I questioned God throughout my wilderness experiences. God, why am I nine years old and don't have a mother or a father? God, why does my grandmother hate me so? God, why is it that everyone who is supposed to love me has been taken away from me? The questions went on and on.

One day, while travelling for work, I was sitting in the lobby of the Omni Hotel in Atlanta, Georgia, and heard God's voice, just as your child hears your voice when you call him or her. "Do you trust me?" "Who do you think carried you through the wilderness?" "Are you not my child?"

I cried like a baby in the middle of the hotel because at that very moment I knew my Heavenly Father was carrying me through the wilderness. All the hurts, lies, failures, and disappointments from family members during my childhood were actually sharpening me. God knew my purpose. Everything I had encountered prepared me to tell a story that would have killed most people. I needed and wanted to share my story so that another woman could see that, despite her wilderness experience, she could come out of that wilderness knowing God never left her and that she survived.

I am grateful and truly blessed that nothing from my past made it into my future for a reason. God had covered me my entire life.

Nikki Giovanni, the well-known African-American poet, once said, "Mistakes are a fact of life. It is the response to the error that counts."

Sisterhood and the Mask

The definition of "sisterhood," according to the *Urban Dictionary* (www.urbandictionary.com), is: "A bond between two or more girls, not always related by blood. They always tell the truth, honor each other, and love each other like sisters."

I hear so many women say, "I don't trust women, so therefore I don't have women friends." When I hear women say these words, I cringe in the soul. Every woman has a story that makes her who she is and that also decides which mask she wears around other women. I had to face my personal truths, learn to walk proudly in my truth, and most importantly, learn to LOVE myself. When I learned to walk boldly in my truth and embrace my scars, which included being a motherless child, suffering molestation, dealing with a father who denied me, and coming to terms with hurtful family, I could remove my mask.

Sister girls, learn to truly love yourselves so you can love other sister girls and see them as extensions of yourselves. We must learn to cover our sisters, and that includes removing the mask so they will see you survived the fire and came out shining like a diamond. I see so many women painting pictures that they've always had it together. How delusional is that, sisters?

Women use the phrase "I am my sister's keeper" too freely. Do they truly understand what that phrase says? It's saying, my sister girl, that when you lack, I got you, and when you can't find the strength to pray for yourself and your situation, I will go before the Lord on your behalf. I will not gossip about you when you have entrusted me with innermost secrets. Sister girls, we have to learn that if another sister hasn't offended us, we must stop gossiping about her, just to try and fit in with other women.

I can't tolerate women who tear down other women based on such things as labels and finances. Only weak women do this. I choose to empower my sister girls. Ladies, when God has delivered you out of the wilderness, rise and bless another sister girl with your story.

I am blessed to have my sister girls, who are everything to me: Bonita, Phyllis, Carolyn, and Yvette. After I had removed my mask, we all cried, hugged, laughed, and bonded. These women are the real deal. They have seen me in my rawness, and they love and cover me daily—and I them. A piece of the woman I am today is largely due to them covering me, for I can still be a hot mess at times.

I can count on Phyllis, the mother of the sister circle, saying, "Steph, you know you're wrong, but you know I love you." I can count on Bonita not ever judging me and always loving my imperfect self while we laugh until our stomachs hurt. Carolyn is my voice of reason; I call her, and everything makes sense. Yvette is my sister who challenges me by asking fifty million questions, such as: "Are you okay, Bossy?" or "Why haven't I heard from you, Bossy?" My sister circle consists of very different women, but they inspire me and hold me accountable to be my best self.

Be Happy. Be Bright. Be You

I was invited by a phenomenal woman by the name of Mrs. Lisa Gibson from my hometown of Chicago to join an awesome women's group called Jewels, which she and her good friend Mrs. Marissa Greaves-Fenton started. My prayer has always been for God to surround me and enlarge my territory with women of substance and faith, ones who will cover their sister girls and have the mindset of "I am my sister's keeper." The vision statement of Jewels is "BE HAPPY. BE BRIGHT. BE YOU." Jewels are passionate women who desire to create an inspiring space that connects beautiful spirits desiring to Live Life On Purpose.

This group of awesome women desires that all women push beyond their limits, find their voices, and exceed their own expectations.

When I was invited into this women's group, the first thing Lisa said to me was, "We do not do mess." My response was, "Thank God, Lisa."

You see, when you pray to God and are serious about this thing called "getting it right," God will direct and order your step exactly where you need to be and will align you with women who will cover you. Ladies, when we connect with other sister girls, we are a FORCE. Pray and ask God for Divine connections.

In the words of my fellow Jewels: "BE HAPPY. BE BRIGHT. BE YOU." Remember to be your authentic self and know you are much more beautiful after you remove the mask. YES, removing the mask makes you vulnerable, but it also frees you to live your best life.

Because God has shown me grace and mercies, I am able to share my testimony of God's goodness.

About Stephanie

Stephanie lives outside of Washington, DC, with her husband, Reginald, but will always be a Chicago girl at heart.

She believes that a woman's gift lies within her life's passion. Stephanie's passion is helping women be all that God has called them to be, as well as helping women understand that their wilderness journey only lasts for a season.

Contact Stephanie at:

sbrenee7@yahoo.com

Friend Stephanie on Facebook:

https://www.facebook.com/stephanie.bullock.735